D1045459

Love Is
Published by Orange, a division of The reThink Group, Inc.
5870 Charlotte Lane, Suite 300
Cumming, GA 30040 U.S.A.
The Orange logo is a registered trademark of The reThink Group, Inc.

All rights reserved. Except for brief excerpts for review purposes, no part of this book may be reproduced or used in any form without written permission from the publisher.

All Scripture quotations, unless otherwise noted, are taken from the *Holy Bible, New International Version®. NIV®.* Copyright © 1973, 1978, 1984 by International Bible Society. Used by permission of Zondervan.

Other Orange products are available online and direct from the publisher. Visit our website at www.WhatIsOrange.org for more resources like these.

ISBN: 978-1-941259-69-6

©2017 The reThink Group, Inc.

Lead Writer: Lauren Terrell
Lead Editor: Mike Jeffries
Project Manager: Nate Brandt
Book Design & Additional Illustration: Jacob Hunt

Printed in the United States of America
First Edition 2017

1 2 3 4 5 6 7 8 9 10

04/28/17

LOVE.

It's a BIG word.

And over the years, this one syllable has been defined dozens
of ways . . .

FLOWERS A VERB
SMILING
FAIRYTALE PINK POWERFUL
VALENTINE UNCONDITIONAL
HEART DEVOTION MUSHY GUSHY
THE ONLY LOVE
ONE I SEE OPEN
DOOR
PATIENT BATTLEFIELD
THE WAY YOU LOOK AT ME
KIND VERY, VERY
LAUGHING
SITTING IN A TREE EXTRAORDINARY
K-I-S-S-I-N-G PRINCE CHARMING RED
MAKES THE WORLD BLIND
GO 'ROUND

But love is more than valentines, fairy tales and Disney movies.

It's actually the main point of the Bible.
The reason people go to church each Sunday.
The purpose of Jesus's life.

4

That's why, if you want to know what Christianity is all about, if you want to follow God and live like Jesus, LOVE is a great place to start.

Believe it or not, when Jesus was a kid like you, He did exactly what you are doing right now. Okay, He didn't read this book because it wasn't written yet. But He wanted to learn more about God and how He fit into God's big story—the same reason you picked up this book!

The Bible doesn't tell us much about Jesus's childhood. The four books of the Bible that tell about Jesus's life (Matthew, Mark, Luke and John) talk a lot about His birth (because, Christmas!) and the three years He spent teaching when He was grown.

But those four books leave out pretty much everything in between.

Except for this one story we find in the second chapter of Luke. It's a short story—only a couple of paragraphs—about Jesus as a 12-year-old boy.

Jesus had gone with His family on a trip to Jerusalem. (Picture that long drive you take to the beach each summer but instead of a car, you're walking beside a camel. And instead of treats from the gas station, you eat stale bread. And instead of it taking eight hours, it takes four days.)

When Jesus's family was ready to pack up and head back home from Jerusalem, they couldn't find 12-year-old Jesus anywhere.

Finally, after Jesus was missing for three days (you don't even want to think about how much trouble you would be in if you disappeared for three whole days) Mary and Joseph found Jesus in the one place they couldn't exactly get mad at Him for being in: The Temple.

Luke 2:46 tells us: *"After three days they found him in the temple courtyard. He was sitting with the teachers. He was listening to them and asking them questions."*

Jesus was one smart kid.

He knew that some things in life were really important. Things like God and Scripture and LOVE. So, He made a point to learn about those things.

Chances are, your life won't look exactly like Jesus's.

You probably won't perform miracles.
You probably wont convince anyone to give up everything to follow you.
You probably won't turn the most powerful people in the world against you.
You probably won't rise from the dead, causing a change in the world so radical millions of people continue to talk about you thousands of years later.

You will make mistakes.

But from this one story in Luke—from these few verses about what Jesus was like as a kid your age—you are off to a great start. You are finding out about the things that matter most in life. You are reading this book!

Hopefully after reading this book, you continue in Jesus's footsteps as much as possible.

If you don't know what that means, check out the last verse in Luke chapter 2: "Jesus became wiser and stronger. He also became more and more pleasing to God and to people."

(You might have also heard this translation of Luke 2:52: "And Jesus grew in wisdom and stature and in favor with God and man.")

There it is. The key to growing up like Jesus.

If you look closely, Jesus did four things as He got older. One of them—becoming stronger—will happen without you trying too hard. Adults are stronger than kids. It's pure biology.

The other three—becoming wiser, more pleasing to God, and more pleasing to people—will take some work.

That's exactly why we wrote this book. Just like Jesus, we want you to get answers to your questions about who God is and what it means to live your life following God. And just like Jesus, we want you to grow up with

WISDOM, FAITH, AND FRIENDSHIPS.

And as it turns out, those three things all come down to understanding one BIG word . . .

LOVE.

WEEK ONE

INTRODUCTION

God. Christian. Bible. Christ. Jesus. Christianity. Religion. Church.

These are either words you have heard so much you can't remember life without them, or they are brand new concepts you are still trying to wrap your brain around.

You probably know these are big, important words. You just aren't sure why they are so important. For you, they might have something to do with . . .

> . . . standing for way too long (and then sitting for way too long) once a week.
>
> . . . those crosses your mom has hung in every corner of your house.
>
> . . . free donuts on Sunday mornings.
>
> . . . why your dad and grandpa can never seem to agree at Thanksgiving.
>
> . . . neckties, tights, and uncomfortable shoes.
>
> . . . seeing how many marshmallows you can fit in your mouth.
>
> . . . Easter candy and Christmas presents!
>
> . . . dying and heaven and hell.

Well, you're right. Those words are related to all these things. But in tiny, itty bitty, insignificant ways. The truth is that Christianity, Jesus, and the Bible are all so much bigger and so much more important than what happens every Sunday morning or the shape of the necklace you wear around your neck.

So this week, we are going to clear up why these words are so important once and for all. (Hint: it has absolutely nothing to do with donuts.)

HUMANS AND HUMANOIDS

From drones to humanoids, from quadcopters to autonomous cars, robots are pretty fascinating to make, watch, and control.

- If you could make a robot, what would it do?

....

- What if you made a humanoid robot exactly like you? Like a robot clone of yourself? What color hair would your robot clone have?

....

- What would its favorite food be?

....

- Where would your robot clone enjoy spending time?

....

- Who would your robot clone like hanging out with?

....

- What would its favorite pastime or hobby be?

....

How cool would it be to make (to have) someone else in this universe who perfectly understands you?

Someone who understands why you love what you love? Who really gets why you hate what you hate? Who wants what you want and acts like you act?

In the book of Genesis—the very first book of the Bible—we are told that God did just that. But instead of making a humanoid exactly like Him, He made a *human* exactly like Him.

So God created human beings in His own likeness. He created them to be like Himself. *(Genesis 1:27a)*

When God created the first humans, Adam and Eve, He made them to be like Him. He created their hearts to love what He loves: joy, kindness, peace, patience, goodness, faithfulness, gentleness, self-control, etc. He created them to despise what he despises: hatred, selfishness, dishonesty, poverty, grief, etc. He created them to be His human likeness on Earth. To rule everything the way God would, if He were a human walking around.

And God didn't stop with Adam and Eve. He kept on creating, human after human, just like Him. Millions of them. Billions.

He made your great grandfather to be like Him.
He made your parents to be like Him.

God made you to be like Him.

And just like you would obsess over that humanoid that loves what you love and hates what you hate, who talks and acts and dresses just like you, God is obsessed with you. But in a really great way. He loves you—His greatest work of art—with the kind of love only a creator can have for His greatest creation.

He desperately wants to be close to you. And He wants you to know Him so you can become even more like Him.

Like programming your robot to know you both love to read, God wants you to be so close to Him that you know you both love making others joyful and showing the world your potential.

God made you.
God made you to be like Him.
God made you to know Him.
God made you.

And because He loves you so much, He made you to be like Him and to know Him. But the story doesn't end there. Like all great stories, God's story gets a lot worse and then a whole lot better.

But for today, spend some time thinking about the ways you might be like God. What characteristics do you have in your heart that you think God also has? List a few of those things here (hint: joyful, empathetic, brave, forgiving, generous).

....

....

....

....

....

....

....

CRUMPLED DREAMS

Find a piece of paper to crumple into a ball. Any piece of paper. Well, except for a page from this book. You should definitely not tear a page out of this book and crumple it into a ball. Hey, please not your homework either.

Okay, find a *scrap* piece of paper and crumple it into a ball. Really squeeze and squish it.

Now open it up and lay it flat again (careful not to tear it).

Does the paper look the same as it did before you crumpled it? How does it look different?

....

....

Is there anything you can do to make the paper look the way it did before? Circle one:

YES   NO

Yesterday, we talked about how *you* are the creation God is most proud of. *You* are made in God's image to love what He loves, to hate what He hates and to act like He acts.

But remember, the story doesn't end there. Remember, God's story gets a lot worse before it gets better.

God created humans—including you—to be like Him, but something happened: The humans God created decided to do something God would never do.

They decided to break God's one rule. That was what He called a sin.

Maybe you grew up hearing the story of Adam and Eve. Maybe you've never heard of them. Maybe you have a vague feeling it has something to do with a snake and some fruit. Here are the basics:

> When God made the first humans, they were perfect, clean, without sin, just like God (kind of like that scrap paper before you crumpled it). But it wasn't long until God's favorite creation broke His heart by doing what they knew was wrong—by sinning.
>
> God told the first humans, Adam and Eve, they could eat the fruit from any tree but one. And what did they do? They ate the fruit from the forbidden tree, of course (humans, right?).
>
> When Adam and Eve broke God's one rule, sin entered the world. And because people were now different from God in this one (huge) way, they were separated from Him *forever*. All of Adam and Eve's children, grandchildren, their great-grandchildren, their great-great grandchildren, their great-great-great (well, you get the idea) . . . they all sinned.

In the Bible, the book of Romans tells us:

> **Everyone has sinned. No one measures up to God's glory.** *(Romans 2:23)*

Sin had entered the world and there was no undoing it (kind of like how you crumpled up that piece of paper and there's no way to make it flat and clean again).

And today, sin is still part of human nature. Adam and Eve and all their great (times infinity) grandchildren aren't the only ones who messed up. Your parents mess up. Your friends mess up. Your teachers, coaches, and family mess up.

You mess up.

Just like the book of Romans says, *everyone* messes up. There are no humans who are exactly like God—as perfect and pure and good as He is. So it's no surprise to God—or anyone else for that matter—when you do mess up. No one expects you to be perfect.

You make bad choices sometimes. You put what you want first, instead of what God wants. You love what you love more than you love what God loves. That's what makes you . . .

    . . . say mean things to your friend.
    . . . disobey your mom or dad.
    . . . throw a fit (and a few remotes) when you lose your game.
    . . . hurt others, yourself, and God.

Those are the things that separate you from God—that make you different from God. And just like you get your TV privileges taken away for refusing to give your sister the remote for the third night in a row, there is a consequence for all your sins . . . death.

Wait. Calm down. God isn't going to kill you for lying to your teacher. All that means is, because humans sin, they don't deserve to be with God after they die. They—we, *you*—deserve to just die and that's it. No heaven. No after party. No angels. Just an eternity of being dead because . . .

. . . you mess up.
. . . you are different from God.
. . . you crumpled the paper.
. . . and there is no way to take it back.
There's no way for you to undo it.

BUT . . .

Yeah, today is going to end with another cliffhanger. But just so you don't feel *too* hopeless and down about the disaster you've made of your crumpled life, here's a hint: God loves you. So much He could *never* stand to be away from you for all of eternity. So hold on until tomorrow because God's story is about to get *a lot* better.

And in the meantime, write down one thing you've done recently that you're really proud of. Could be a grade you've earned, something kind you did for someone, a brilliant idea you had or tons of other awesome-ness.

....

....

....

....

....

....

....

....

See? You aren't all bad!

SET IT STRAIGHT

Has someone ever done something that really, really, really hurt you? Something that was so big, so mean, you were sure your relationship would never be the same?

- What happened?

....

....

- How did you feel?

....

....

- Were you able to move past it? Did that someone apologize and make things right again?

....

....

You are probably *dying* (okay, maybe that's a bad word to use here) for what comes next in God's story. Yesterday ended pretty grim. Humans sin. You mess up. And there's nothing you can do to fix it.

BUT . . .

. . . there *is* something God can do (and *did* do) to fix it. That's right, you are created by a God whose love for you is powerful enough to totally undo all your sins—to take that crumpled up piece of paper (remember that from yesterday?) and make it absolutely flawless again. That doesn't mean you won't mess it up again, BUT because of Jesus, God will forgive you over and over.

How great is that?!?!

Just a few paragraphs down from the verse we talked about yesterday, the Bible says this:

> But here is how God has shown His love for us: While we were still sinners, Christ died for us. (Romans 5:8)

That may not seem that great. Christ, Jesus, God's Son died . . . how's that supposed to make us feel better about all this talk about death? Just seems to add more death to this crumpled mess.

Let's break it down . . .

God made humans.
Humans messed up.
The consequence for messing up is death—being separated from God forever.

BUT . . .

God sent Jesus.
Jesus, Christ, God's own Son was born and lived a sinless life on earth.
Jesus still died (even though He didn't sin).
And Jesus rose from the dead.

That last part is the most important. Jesus beat death. When Jesus rose from the dead, He made a way for us—for *you*—to be with God in Heaven. When Jesus rose from the dead, He made things right again between God and humans once and for all.

That's how much God loves you.

You hurt others BUT . . . . . . **God loves you.**
You break His rules BUT . . . **God loves you.**
You mess up BUT . . . . **God loves you.**

God loves you SO much that while humans were still sinners, still messing up, He sent Jesus to make things right—to make sure YOU could be with Him again one day.

Pretty great, right?

One of the coolest things about God making things right between us and Him is . . . *He* was the one to do it. Think about that person who hurt you—that person who messed up so big, you didn't think things would ever be the same. Now, who do you think should be the one to set things straight? That other person, right? You would think . . .

BUT . . .

God was the one that set things straight between Him and us. We messed up. We separated ourselves from God forever. But He knew there was no way we could fix it. So He sent Jesus. We were the ones to mess things up. And He was the One who made it right again.

Because . . . **God loves you.**

Spend a few minutes today writing a note to God explaining how this makes you feel. Maybe you feel grateful. Maybe you feel confused. Maybe you feel relieved, overjoyed, or even sad. Reach out and write your thoughts to God. He loves you and would love to hear from you.

Dear God,

When I think about You making up for all the times I mess up, I feel . . .

THE GREATEST GIFT

What are some of the coolest gifts you have ever gotten, or could ever hope to get?

....

....

Now, picture those things wrapped in bright paper with ribbons and massive bows sitting right outside your front door, just waiting for you to bring them in and rip into them. Or waiting for you to run outside and rip into them (if you are imagining a full-sized helicopter or something).

But . . . instead, you leave them there—waiting outside your front door.

Day after day, you step around them on your way to school, nudge them out of the way when you run outside to play with friends, shrug your shoulders when your friend points up at the massive helicopter-shaped present and asks, "Dude, are you ever going to open that?"

That's pretty unlikely to happen. Because—hello!—you are wasting days you could be arriving at school in a *helicopter!* And if you are like every other person who has ever lived, when you see something wrapped in shiny paper with a massive bow, your hands start tingling with excitement to *open it already!*

The Bible tells us that God has given each of us a gift and believe it or not, it's actually way better than a personal helicopter (or any of the other gifts you wrote up there). But instead of having to rip off wrapping paper, ribbons and bows, all you have to do to get God's gift is . . . *believe it.*

So, what could be better than any gift you could possibly imagine?

Jesus.

Okay, okay. Maybe you have heard that before. Or maybe you haven't and are currently giving this book the "you crazy" look. Maybe you're thinking, "Jesus is really great and all but . . .*my own helicopter.*"

So hear this out. Unscrunch your nose and take a minute to think about these questions honestly:

Can a helicopter (or any other gift you could imagine) . . .

> . . . be there to really listen to you any time of day?
> . . . love you when it feels like no one else does?
> . . . want to be near you when you have messed up big time?
> . . . give you joy when life seems unbelievably awful?
> . . . show you how to become the kind of person
> everyone wants to be around?
> . . . help you choose the right kind of people to
> spend time with?
> . . . give you life even after you die?

The gift God gave us when Jesus died and then... *un*-died (whoa)... isn't like any other gift you could imagine. It isn't something you can unwrap and spend thrilling hours playing with. But it also isn't something that will get old, boring and tossed in the donation pile one day.

God's gift grows and morphs with you for the rest of your life. It shifts and changes into exactly what you need it to be in the moment. It's unexplainable **peace**, when you have every right to be freaking out. It's **wisdom** to make the best choice in the very moment you need it the most. It's **joy** in place of jealousy, **patience** in place of frustration and **love** in place of hate.

And if all that weren't enough, when our lives end on earth, God's gift gives us another life with Him in Heaven.

So, okay, God's gift to you *might* be a little better than a personal helicopter. But . . . you can't unwrap it. You can't pick it up and bring it in your front door. So how do you accept this gift?

In the Bible, John 3:16 says,

> **God so loved the world that He gave His one and only Son. Anyone who believes in Him will not die but will have eternal life.**

It's right there. In the beginning of the second sentence. The key to God's gift: *Anyone who believes.*

God gives His great gift to anyone who believes. And because . . .

. . . Jesus was God's Son,
. . . Jesus lived in a way only God's Son could live,
. . . Jesus died and rose from the dead,

. . . you can believe.

Because of Jesus, you can believe.

God made you. You mess up. God loves you. And **you can believe** God's story. You can believe God's plan for your life. You can believe God wants the best for you on this earth and in heaven.

If you think you do believe what the Bible says is true, if you would like to have a relationship with Jesus, to be able to turn to Him and lean on Him always, if you believe, take a minute to turn to page 30 and follow the "What's Next" section.

If it all seems a little too new, a little too good to be true, a little too fantastical, that's okay for now! Keep reading with us. Page 32 will be there for you when you are ready to believe.

THE BILLION-DOLLAR QUESTION

What would you do with one billion dollars? It's an age-old question you might already have an answer for, but if you haven't figured it out already, you probably should because . . . you never know.

Actually, you can be pretty certain you will never be handed a billion dollars, but it's fun to dream! Take a few minutes to write out your billion-dollar plan here:

....

....

....

If someone walked up to you and handed you one billion dollars in cash, it would change everything about your life, wouldn't it?

It would change the stuff you bought (hello, *all* the hoverboards in the world). It would change your summer vacations (hello, private islands). It would even change the lives of the people around you (hello, end of world hunger).

Well, just like a gift of one billion dollars would radically change your life, God's gift is meant to radically change your life.

When Jesus lived on this earth, He radically changed the way people thought about God, themselves, and others. Before Jesus came around, people tried to follow over six *hundred* laws to stay on God's good side. Things like, "Never pick grapes up off the ground," and "Never wear clothes made of a mix of wool and linen." (Say what?!) It was hard to keep them all straight.

Then Jesus came and changed everything. He threw out all the laws and made it simple. Instead of it being about 613 things, He made it all about one thing: LOVE.

Check out what Jesus says in the book of Matthew when one of the religious leaders asks Him which of the laws are most important:

> **"'Teacher,' he asked, 'which is the most important commandment in the Law?' Jesus replied, 'Love the Lord your God with all your heart and with all your soul. Love Him with all your mind. This is the first and most important commandment. And the second is like it. Love your neighbor as you love yourself. Everything that is written in the Law and the Prophets is based on these two commandments.'"**
> **(Matthew 22:36-40)**

Love. Love. Love. (This is where the book starts to get a little mushy.)

But really, Jesus was saying it's not about remembering 613 laws.
It's about *love.*
It's about loving God.
It's about loving others.
It's about loving yourself.

Love changes everything.

Think about it. Would you rather someone treated you kindly because they love you or because it's the law? Because of love, obviously.

Love changes everything.

And get this: because God loves you SO much (like we talked about a couple days ago), you have His love in you and you are capable of loving the way Jesus loved during His time on earth.

Jesus did a lot more during His time here than just fix things between God and the entire human race (as if that wasn't enough). He also showed us practical ways to:

1. **Love God** (praying, obeying, sharing His story with others, etc.)
2. **Love others** (serving, giving, helping, etc.)
3. **Love ourselves** (discovering your talents, protecting your heart, knowing how awesome you are, etc.)

Like Jesus said, all the laws of following and having a relationship with God come down to love. And when you believe God's story and decide to follow Him, it changes everything. **Love changes everything.**

Take a few minutes to think about how the three kinds of love Jesus talks about could change everything. Think through the following situations you might face:

LOVE GOD: You want to go to your friend's Saturday-night slumber party, but your little brother is getting baptized at church the same Sunday morning and it would be too early to ask your friends parents to take you home. Plus, you'd be waking up after a massive pillow fight. Skipping church is an option, but because you **love God**, you . . .

....

....

....

LOVE OTHERS: Your class trip is coming up but one of your classmates (the one you never talk to because, earwax much?!) can't afford to go. The whole grade will be on this incredible overnight trip but *one* person. You might turn a blind eye and pretend you don't notice, but because you **love others**, you . . .

....

....

....

....

....

LOVE YOURSELF: Two of your friends are really good at soccer—like, incredible—but every time you play with them, you kick the ball out of bounds or forget you aren't supposed to grab the soccer ball with your hands. Your self-esteem is starting to take a hit, but because you **love yourself**, you . . .

....

....

....

....

....

If you are reading this page, that means you're ready to open God's incredible gift by believing!

WOO HOO!!! YIP YIP YIPEE!!!

All week, we talked about the basics of God's big story that began with what's written in the Bible and is continuing on even today.

We talked about how God loved you before you were even born. He created you in His Image. And He loves you right now.

But there is something that separates us from Him, something that keeps us from being with Him forever. It's called sin. It's the stuff we do wrong. Sin keeps us from living out the story that God wants for us.

On our own, we can't do anything about this. We need God to step in and help. But because God loves us, He made a way for all of us to live with Him forever.

PAUSE

WHAT IS SIN? ....

....

HAVE YOU EVER SINNED? ....

WHEN? ....

....

WHAT IS THE PROBLEM WITH SIN? ....

....

God gave up the most important, valuable, and perfect thing He had—Jesus—for you because He knew sin would keep you from living with Him forever.

We are apart from God and would stay that way, but because God loves us, He gave His son to fix that relationship. Jesus came to make a way for you to be in God's story.

And Jesus gave up His life on the cross to pay for our sins. Three days later, Jesus rose from the dead! His resurrection defeated death and makes a relationship with God possible again.

PAUSE

WHAT DID GOD GIVE US?..

....

WHY DID GOD GIVE THIS GIFT?...

....

WHAT DID JESUS DO FOR US?..

....

When you receive a gift what do you do? You open it. God said you could open His gift by believing.

Believing simply means to trust. It's a lot like sitting in a chair. When you sit in a chair, you put all your weight in it. You trust that it will hold you up. That's what it's like to believe in or to trust in God's gift.

To open the gift God gave you, you trust Jesus with your whole life and rest in the fact that He died and rose again for you.

PAUSE

WHAT DOES IT MEAN TO TRUST IN SOMETHING?

....

....

HOW DO YOU KNOW GOD LOVES YOU?

....

....

WRITE (OR SIMPLY PRAY) a prayer to God telling Him why you need Him, how grateful you are for His gift and how you want Him to teach you to obey His commands and love like He loves.

....

....

....

....

....

....

....

So... do you feel completely different?! Has everything around you magically changed?

Probably not.

God's gift of trusting in Him and having a relationship with Jesus *will* change everything. But it takes constant work on your part, like every other relationship. In order for God's love to change everything, you have to learn a little more about God and His humongous love. And the two best ways to do that are:

○ **Tell a grownup you trust and who loves Jesus (and you) about your decision to believe and open God's gift!**

○ **Read the rest of this book to learn more about God's love.**

WEEK TWO

INTRODUCTION

Have you ever had to make a decision?

Of course you have. Every single day, we are all faced with options, choices, and decisions.

From small things like: Cheerios or Frosted Mini Wheats?

To really big things like: Go for the next belt in karate or make more time for friends and school?

Life is complicated. And sometimes even the smallest decisions have you staring at the open pantry in a near-panic.

The good news is, this is one of the ways God's love changes everything. No, there's nothing in the Bible about cereal or black belts. But when you know what God loves, it's easier to know which decisions really matter. When you know what God loves, you have a clearer idea of what God wants for you.

Remember the intro way back on page 4? We talked about four ways Jesus grew over the years from the 12-year-old kid who skipped out on the family vacay to sit with priests, to the Teacher and Leader who rose from the dead and started a new world religion.

Luke 2:52 (NIRV) says:

"Jesus became wiser . . ."

Jesus knew God as much as anyone could. He was God's *Son* after all. So He knew what God loved. He also knew what God said was best. And that made Him wiser. That changed the way He made decisions.

The same is true for you. When you know what God says is best, you will make decisions based on God's plan for you.

AND WHEN YOU ARE MAKING THE DECISIONS YOU KNOW ARE BEST FOR GOD'S PLAN FOR YOU, YOU'LL FIND IT EASIER TO LOVE YOURSELF. AND WHEN YOU LOVE YOURSELF, YOU'LL FIND IT EASIER TO MAKE THE DECISIONS YOU KNOW ARE BEST FOR THAT PLAN GOD HAS FOR YOU.

PRETTY COOL LITTLE CYCLE, HUH?

So let's jump right in and spend this week learning how to love yourself like God loves you . . . through the decisions you make every day. (Starting with Lucky Charms. Everyone needs a good dehydrated marshmallow every now and then.)

TREASURE HUNT

We've all heard stories about hidden treasure. Some are fantasies. Some are myths or ancient legends rooted in a truth from the past.

But did you know there are real-life hidden treasures out there today?

No joke.

There's a 42-pound box of treasure hidden by a man named Forrest Fenn in the 1980s somewhere in the mountains north of Santa Fe, New Mexico, worth approximately $2 million.

In the early 1800s, a man named Thomas Beale came across $63 million of gold in the Rocky Mountains. When he died, he left a code for his family to find the treasure, but the cipher has never been solved!

In 1622, a fleet of Spanish ships sunk off the coast of Key West, Florida, carrying over $700 million in treasures. About 30 years ago, real-life treasure hunter Mel Fisher actually found $500 million of the Spanish treasure, leaving over $200 million left to be discovered.

But hold on a sec. Before you Google "Forrest Fenn," book a trip to the Rockies, or start your scuba diving lessons, check out these verses found in the book of Proverbs:

> **Let your ears listen to wisdom. Apply your heart to understanding. Call out for the ability to be wise. Cry out for understanding. Look for it as you would look for silver.** Search for it as you would search for hidden treasure. **Then you will understand how to have respect for the Lord. You will find out how to know God.** (Proverbs 2:2-5)

I know, I know. It's a hard sell to say *wisdom* is as valuable as a sunken treasure worth $200 million. But the longer you live your life in a relationship with Jesus, the more you'll see that the Bible is pretty much always right.

Right now, you're thinking of mansions made of solid gold, private planes, birthday parties hosted by Taylor Swift, Ferraris made just to your liking and an endless supply of front row tickets to all the concerts, play-offs, and performances you can imagine.

So let me ask you a few questions:

Can any amount of money . . .

> . . . fix your relationship with your best friend?
> . . . make you feel proud of the person you are?
> . . . bring you continuous love, joy, peace, patience,
> kindness, goodness, faithfulness, gentleness,
> and self-control (all the qualities that make *life* rich)?

These are some of the things wisdom brings. Wisdom is not only the ability to make the *right* choice. It's the knowledge needed to make the *best* choice—the *wisest* choice—in every situation.

Sure, you could pay your friend a few million dollars to be your friend again. But the friendship wouldn't be *genuine*. You could feel proud of all your Ferrari, but Ferraris don't say anything great about your *character*. And you would find temporary peace and joy each time you bought out another toy section, but that joy would fade with time (and battery life).

Wisdom is the only way to get to the *real* treasures of life. That's why the Bible tells us to search for it as you would *search for hidden treasure*.

There's not much point in wasting your time searching for Forrest Fenn's treasure. (At least four people have gone missing while searching and still no one has found it.)

Instead, spend your time searching for a treasure you are sure to find, a treasure guaranteed to bring contentment. That treasure is wisdom. **Wisdom is worth searching for.**

This week, we are going to talk about some very practical ways to search for wisdom. But first, you have to believe **wisdom is worth searching for.** You have to decide it is even more valuable than hidden treasure.

What are three things you can think of that cannot be bought with money, but can only come with wisdom?

1.
....

2.
....

3.
....

AN EXPERT

Match the talent on the left with the expert on the right . . .

IF YOU WANTED
TO LEARN TO . . .

YOU WOULD SEEK
ADVICE FROM . . .

Cook	a teacher
Tumble	an author
Garden	a sketch artist
Read	a nurse
Write a novel	a physical trainer
Draw	a botanist
Fly a plane	a nutritionist
Walk on the moon	a gymnast
Draw blood	a pilot
Eat well	a chef
Exercise	an astronaut

When you want to perfect that difficult basketball move, you get help from your friend who's had it down for months (not someone just barely able to reach the hoop).

When you want to know how to get to the next level in your favorite video game, you ask your friend who has mastered all the levels to show you (not your great aunt who doesn't know the difference between a play station and a PlayStation).

When you are trying something new, something you aren't quite sure how to do, it makes the most sense to seek advice from people who are already experts, professionals, or at least better than you at it.

The book of Proverbs has a lot to say about wisdom (which makes sense because most of it was written by King Solomon who was widely known as the wisest man who had ever lived).

> The way of foolish people seems right to them. But those who are wise listen to advice. *(Proverbs 12:15)*

In the book of Proverbs, King Solomon points out the tricky-ness of wisdom. According to King Solomon, it's easy to think that only your way, your opinions, your desires, preferences, and ideas are wise if you don't ask for advice from others.

But that's foolish.

Foolish. That's a pretty strong word for the Bible. But if you want wisdom, if you want to be wise, you have to look for *and* listen to others' advice.

If you decided yesterday that wisdom was more valuable than any hidden treasure and worth searching for, that's a huge first step. So the next step is . . . to start searching!

And where better to start your search for the treasure of wisdom than by finding the people who have already found it?

In order to get wisdom and be a wise person, you can't simply rely on your own idea of what is wise. And you definitely can't ask others you know who aren't very wise to begin with. (You know exactly who I'm talking about.)

Instead, find people—usually people who are older than you, but not always—who seem to consistently make wise choices. You know, someone who always seems to always be on the best side of a situation. **Find someone wiser than you.**

King Solomon knew that no matter how much wisdom you find, you aren't truly wise until you know you can't rely completely on your own wisdom.

Confused?

It's like that mind game: The only rule is to not think of the game. If you think of the game, you lose the game. (Go ahead. Try to win. I bet you just lost.)

Proverbs says wisdom is similar. The moment you think you are the wisest person you know, you are no longer very wise. In order to be wise, you have to always **find someone wiser than you.**

Pretty cool first clue to finding the most valuable treasure on earth, huh?

Take a minute to think of three people in your life who are wiser than you. Write their names here and remember to go to them next time you need a little advice or wisdom:

1.
....
2.
....
3.
....

SUPERNATURAL WISDOM

Before you read today's devotion, find a quiet place—somewhere you can't hear the sounds of your brother's video game, or the guys talking outside, or somewhere you won't be asked about homework, dishes, or walking the dog.

I'll wait.

You there? Great!

Now, I'm going to ask you to start today off by praying. Not yet! When I say go, mark this page, close your eyes and picture God quietly sitting next to you, listening. Then pray a simple prayer asking God to be with you in your heart and mind throughout today's devotion and the rest of the day.

It doesn't have to be a fancy prayer. There are no right or wrong words. Just you turning to God and focusing on Him for a minute.

Okay . . . GO!

PRAYER BREAK

Great! Now, let me ask you a few questions . . .

Where do you go to get . . .

    Shoes? ....

    Hamburgers? ....

    Toys? ....

    Pizza? ....

    Games? ....

    Candy? ....

    Swimsuits? ....

    Wisdom? ....

That last one might be a little difficult. Wisdom isn't something you can buy. It's not something you can carry home with you and place on a table next to your bed. So how do you *get* or *have* something that you can't see or hold?

In the Bible, the book of James tell us:

> **If any of you needs wisdom, you should ask God for it. He will give it to you. God gives freely to everyone and doesn't find fault. (James 1:5)**

James, *who happens to be the little brother of Jesus,* tells us to **ask God for wisdom.** Think about that for a second. What would it take for you to believe your brother is actually God Himself? And not only that, but to advise people to pray to *your big brother* for wisdom?

James must have really known it worked firsthand. He must have truly experienced the wisdom God gives when you ask in order to tell others, "Hey, it actually works. When you ask God for wisdom, He'll give it to you!"

Something happens in your heart and mind when you pray. Prayer changes how you see things.

That's why we started today's devotion with a prayer. You probably felt a little calmer after your prayer, more focused. You may even notice a difference in the way you interact with others, the way you handle disappointments or the way you look at problems today.

In the same way that prayer has the power to change the way you look at life, praying to **ask God for wisdom** has the power to help you make the *best* choices for you, everyone around you and for God's story.

You may not hear God's voice saying, "Go with the brown shirt, not the red one" or "That sleepover is going to be bad news" but the best choice—the wise choice—will seem a little clearer. God will give you the wisdom to know which path is best for you.

Give it a try over the next few days. When you can't figure out the wisest choice, turn to God. **Ask God for wisdom.** Then, use the space on page 51 to write about a situation in which you needed wisdom and the wisdom God gave you.

I needed wisdom in . . .

....

....

....

....

....

....

....

The wisdom God gave me was . . .

....

....

....

....

....

....

....

POP QUIZ!

Quick! Answer these questions (no Googling!):

- How many hairs are on the average human head?

  ....

- Where is the tallest tree in the world?

  ....

- How long is the Great Wall of China?

  ....

- What is the most poisonous snake in the world?

  ....

- Why do people yawn?

  ....

Chances are, you got 0/0 on that (slightly unfair) pop quiz.

In order to know the answers to all that, you would have to talk with a biologist, a botanist, a zoologist . . . or, you know, just Google it.

Yesterday you learned that God is the expert in all things related to wisdom. But did you know the Bible—God's Word—is the Google of the wisdom world?

That's right. When you aren't sure what to do, when you need to know the wise choice, you can "Bible it" (get it? like, "Google it" but . . . okay, okay, you get it. Maybe it wasn't the *wisest* pun). Just check out what the Bible says in the book of 2 Timothy.

God has breathed life into all Scripture. It is useful for teaching us what is true. It is useful for correcting our mistakes. It is useful for making our lives whole again. It is useful for training us to do what is right.
(2 Timothy 3:16)

"Training us to do what is right." That's what wisdom is: Knowing (and doing) what is right. And this verse from Timothy tells us that if we **discover what the Bible says,** we will find wisdom.

But it's kind of hard to discover everything that 66 books, over two thousand pages, nearly one million words, has to say!

The Bible is a *long* book. Made up of a lot of little books. With a lot of big wisdom. And when you have a problem that needs immediate wisdom, it's hard to know which part of the Bible to turn to.

That's why it's important to start now—before a problem arises.

Because when you **discover what the Bible says,** it tends to pop back up in your head in the most convenient ways.

When you are arguing over the biggest half of the cookie . . .
When you are deciding whom to invite to your birthday party . . .
When you really want to roll your eyes at your mom . . .

God's Word will replay in your mind then, because you took the time to discover it now.

DAY 4

Take some time to discover and read the following verses and write down the piece of wisdom you might get from them.

VERSE: A PIECE OF WISDOM:

Ephesians 4:29-32

....

....

Micah 6:8

....

....

Philippians 2:14

....

....

Luke 10:30-37

....

....

Matthew 7:12

....

....

Philippians 1:9-10

....

....

Psalm 1:1

....

....

Matthew 5:44

....

....

And if you are interested in discovering more of God's wisdom, we suggest starting with reading some of the following books: Matthew, Proverbs, Psalms, Job, or Ecclesiastes.

JUST DO IT

See if you can come up with the answers to these tricky riddles:

- What has a face and two hands, but no arms or legs?

....

- What has to be broken before you can use it?

....

- What has a single eye, but cannot see?

....

- What is something you can never fully have, you can always find someone with more of it than you, you must keep asking for it and if you don't use it, you never had it to begin with?

....

Alright, you caught me. I made that last one up myself. Any guesses?

Think really hard . . .

Did you guess **WISDOM?**

You're right!! (That was pretty *wise* of you).

Think about it. You can never have all the wisdom because there's always someone wiser than you. There's always more wisdom to discover in God's word. And if you stop asking God for it, you'll stop having it at all.

And as you'll learn today, it's not enough to just have wisdom.
It's not enough to simply know what's wise.
You have to *use* your wisdom.
Otherwise, you never really had it.

Confused? That's okay. Check out what Jesus says to His followers in the book of Matthew:

> "So then, everyone who hears my words and puts them into practice is like a wise man. He builds his house on the rock. The rain comes down. The water rises. The winds blow and beat against that house. But it does not fall. It is built on the rock. But everyone who hears my words and does not put them into practice is like a foolish man. He builds his house on sand. The rain comes down. The water rises. The winds blow and beat against that house. And it falls with a loud crash."
> (Matthew 7:24-27)

Maybe you've heard this comparison before. Maybe you know the song (and the hand motions) that go along with it. Or maybe it's brand new to you. Either way, let's break down what Jesus is saying.

Jesus is saying there's a lot of wisdom in His words. But His words alone won't help you when the storms of life come.

People you thought were your friends exclude you.
Your parents get in a fight.
You forget to study for your spelling test.
Someone you love gets really sick.

That's when you have to put His words into practice. You have to know what Jesus taught and DO it. You have to know what is written in God's word and **DO what God says.**

Otherwise, everything will come crumbling down, as if you didn't know God's wisdom in the first place.

Spend the next few minutes completing this story with words or pictures in the boxes provided. Decide what the wise thing to do is, what the *best* choice would be. (Hint: if you don't know, try out some of your new wisdom-finding skills: Ask someone wiser, ask God, or look in the Bible!)

In the first set of boxes, write or draw what might happen if Jonah only knows what's wise but doesn't DO it. In the second set of boxes, write or draw what might happen if Jonah knows and DOES what is wise:

Jonah's best friend, Mason, came over to ride bikes. Mason forgot his helmet and pads. Mason says it's no big deal. He can ride without them. But Jonah's mom has warned him many times how dangerous it can be to ride his bike without safety gear. Jonah and Mason really want to ride their bikes at the same time . . .

1.

2.

Oh, and if you're like me and have to know the answers to those riddles on the top of page 54 here they are: 1. A clock, 2. An egg, 3. A needle

This week, you got clues that took you on a hunt for the most valuable treasure you could ever find: Wisdom.

But you also learned that wisdom is a tricky treasure.

In order to find it, you have to know someone with *more* of it.
You have to constantly ask someone else (God) for it.
The moment you stop looking for it, you lose it.
The only way you can truly have it is to *use* it.

So while you have technically finished a week-long treasure hunt for wisdom, and I should say, "Congratulations," you are really at the beginning of a life-long search for this valuable treasure.

So use this graphic to help you not only remember that wisdom is worth searching for, but to help you remember *how* to find it when you need it most.

Cut out this treasure map. If you have access to a laminator, laminate this picture to protect it and keep it in a special place, or frame it with a small picture frame and keep it in your room where you can see it.

WISDOM
IS WORTH SEARCHING FOR

FIND
SOMEONE
WISER THAN
YOU

ASK GOD
FOR WISDOM

DISCOVER
WHAT THE
BIBLE SAYS

X
WISDOM

N
W ⊙ E
S

DO WHAT
GOD SAYS

WEEK THREE

INTRODUCTION

Do you have any brothers or sisters? How about cousins?
Classmates? Teammates?

The thing with having siblings (or cousins or classmates or
teammates) is that there's always someone who *really* cares if you
get along, if you all treat each other well. It's usually your parent
(or grandparent, or teacher, or coach).

And just like parents (or grandparents or teachers or coaches) love
all their kids equally and want them to all be treated with love and
respect, *God* loves all His children the same. *God* wants them to
all be treated with love and respect.

Think about it. You have probably heard that God loves you
(you've already heard it half a dozen times in this book) but did
you know there are other people reading this book? There are
other people being told, "God loves you." Because, God does.
God loves you. And just like He loves *you*, He loves every other
person He ever made or ever *will* make.

Kind of mind-blowing, huh?

And because God loves everyone, He wants everyone to get along
(just like your mom or your grandpa or your teacher or your coach).

No, that doesn't mean God is going to "pull this car over" if you lose it on your BFF.

But it does mean that when you encounter God's love, when you believe and put your trust in Him, He will give you the ability to see—and love—others in a whole new way.

Remember that verse we talked about at the beginning of the book and then again before Week Two? That's right, we're not done with it, yet. There are two more ways Jesus (the 12-year-old) grew into Jesus (the Savior). As a kid, Jesus got to know everything there was to know about God. He lived His life perfectly, based on what God wanted for Him and because of that, the book of Luke tells us,

"Jesus became wiser and stronger. He also became more and more pleasing to God and to people."
(Luke 2:52)

This week, we are going to focus on that last one: how having a relationship with Jesus can make your relationships better—how God's love can change the way you **love others.**

SOMEONE ELSE'S SHOES

What is your favorite . . .

. . . color? ....

. . . ice cream flavor? ....

. . . subject in school? ....

. . . movie? ....

. . . book? ....

. . . game? ....

. . . way to be treated? ....

Chances are, your answers to the first six questions look different from somebody else who might be reading this book. Maybe a few people all like the same color. But do they *also* like the same ice cream? *And* the same book? Unlikely.

But what *is* likely is that every single person reading this book and every single person who has ever answered the seventh question have all answered in a similar way.

Let me guess. You wrote down that you like to be treated . . .

> . . . well?
> . . . kindly?
> . . . nicely?
> . . . friendly?
> . . . with love?

That's because everyone—no matter what movie or game they think is best, no matter what subject in school is their favorite—*everyone* wants to be treated the same way.

Everyone wants to feel . . .

> . . . liked.
> . . . loved.
> . . . respected.
> . . . valuable.
> . . . important.
> . . . capable.
> . . . talented.

Everyone wants to be treated with *kindness*. Check out what the book of Luke says in the Bible:

> **"Do to others as you want them to do to you."**
> **(Luke 6:31)**

You may have heard a saying like this before. It's called the *Golden Rule*. But did you know it actually comes from the Bible?

You learn something new every day!

This verse—*The Golden Rule*, also known as *empathy*—is a huge first step in having the kind of relationships God wants for you. It's an easy way to figure out how God wants you to treat others.

Should you invite her to your birthday party?
Would you want to be invited?

Should you give him his eraser back?
Would you want your eraser back?

Should you tell everyone about his parents fighting?
Would you want someone to tell such things about your family?

Should you tell her you like her new haircut?
Would you want a compliment on your hair?

Should you forgive him for kicking you?
Would you want to be forgiven?

Should you apologize for losing her favorite book?
Would you want an apology?

It can be hard to put yourself in someone else's shoes but that is the trick to understanding this verse. When you begin to treat others the way you want to be treated, your relationships—with your parents, brothers, sisters, friends, coaches, even enemies—will become the kind of relationships God wants for you.

And when you have a relationship with God, when you are connected with Him, you will find it much easier to **treat others the way you want to be treated.**

Take a few minutes today to answer the following questions:

When was the last time you treated someone *differently* than you would have liked to be treated? What happened?

....

....

....

....

....

....

....

How *should* you have treated that person if you were thinking of how you would like to be treated?

....

....

....

....

....

....

....

SALTY WORDS

Before you start today's devotion, go to your kitchen and find the following things. (You may need to ask an adult to help you.)

- Two eggs
- Two measuring cups (each filled with 1½ cups of warm water)
- 1/3 cup of table salt
- Spoon

I'll wait . . .
Don't mind me . . .
Just humming the *Jeopardy* music in my head . . .

Oh, you're back? Great! Let's get started.

Take a good look at how many grains of salt make up that 1/3 cup of table salt. Each of those grains of salt represents a kind word, compliment, or encouragement.

Then, pour the entire 1/3 cup of salt into one of the containers of water. Use the spoon to stir (and stir and stir and stir and then maybe ask somebody else to stir a little, while you rest your arm) until the salt is completely dissolved.

Now, pick up one of the eggs (that represents a big ol' insult) and drop it—without cracking it!—into the other container of water... (the one with no grains of encouragement . . . AKA salt . . . stirred in).

Pick up the second egg and place it in the container of water filled with kind words (salt).

Did the eggs do the same thing in both containers of water? What happened to the two eggs?

....

....

....

....

If all went right, the first big ol' insult (egg) sunk down deep into the person (container) with no grains of encouragement (salt). And the second big ol' insult (egg) sat right on top—not sinking in deep at all—of the person filled with pieces of encouragement and kind words (salt).

Negative comments, insults, cruel words are a lot heavier—they sink deeper and hurt more—when you haven't heard enough positive comments, compliments, and encouragement to combat them.

In fact, studies show if you hear one negative comment, you need five positive ones to combat it.

In other words, for every . . .
"You're really not that great at math, are you?"

You need five . . .
"You're a great friend."
"Thank you for saving me a seat,"
"I could tell you worked really hard at practice today."
"I love that you're someone I can count on."
"I appreciate your help after school."

So . . . what does this mean about the words you say to others?

Check out what Paul in his letter to the church at Ephesus says about the importance of our words:

> **"Say only what will help to build others up and meet their needs. Then what you say will help those who listen."** *(Ephesians 4:29b)*

It's so easy for us to say the negative things we think. Yet it's hard sometimes to say the positive things we think.

Sometimes it's easier to use our words to make fun of someone than it is to use our words to tell someone why we think they are so great.

But God wants us to love others, to help build others up, and to have strong, genuine friendships. He wants your friends to feel safe with you and know you will say kind things to them, not mean things about them.

And when you have a relationship with God and when you feel and experience God's love for you, you'll find it much easier to **encourage others with your words.**

Over the next few days, practice speaking all your nice thoughts. Even if that kid has heard he's brilliant four times already today or she has been told her soccer header is out of this world three times, he still just got called a freak and she just overheard someone making fun of her backpack.

You never know when someone needs your encouraging words to help combat the negative ones they just heard. You can help keep those unkind words from sinking too deep.

Come back to this page and write down the times you **encourage others with your words** over the next few days here:

....

....

....

....

....

....

....

....

....

....

....

....

....

....

....

....

....

....

....

LET IT GO

Pop quiz!

Circle the heaviest of these three things:

A FEATHER   AN ELEPHANT   A GRUDGE

If you circled the elephant, you either don't know what a grudge is, have never held one, or haven't been in school long enough to recognize a trick question.

A grudge means to feel angry towards someone for some reason.

Of course an elephant is heavier than a feather, but if you have ever held a grudge or had one held against you, you know there is nothing heavier than a grudge.

It weighs you down emotionally.
It keeps you from laughing with your friends.
It won't let you do, think, or talk about much other than your anger.
It's heavy stuff.

Because when you hold a grudge, you are holding on to your anger. Someone once said that holding on to anger is like drinking poison and waiting for the other person to get sick.

Seems pretty crazy, huh?

But that's what we expect when we stay angry with someone. Maybe your mom refused to let you go to your friend's sleepover because you didn't clean your room the right way. Maybe your friend didn't invite you to the sleepover in the first place. Maybe it has nothing to do with a sleepover and you are mad because you didn't get chosen to be on the basketball team this year.

At the time it feels unfair and just about the worst thing that could ever happen to you. And you are going to make the person who hurt you pay by . . . feeling angry and hurt for weeks, even *months*. Wait . . . what?

I hate to be the one to break it to you, but your mom probably has no clue you are even still upset about the whole clean-clothes-shoved-under-your-bed disaster.

Your friends on the basketball team have probably already forgotten you even tried out in the first place.

The only person your poisonous grudge is hurting . . . is *you*. Check out this bit of wisdom from Proverbs 17:9:

> **"Whoever wants to show love forgives a wrong.**
> **But those who talk about it separate close friends."**

Between those two options, it will be pretty easy to guess what God wants us to do: Forgive.

If there is one thing you have learned from this book, it's that God is all about love. Love. Love. Love. (See the title!)

And God wants you to show love by **forgiving and letting go.** If showing others the kind of love that comes from God isn't enough to make you let your anger go, remember when you **forgive and let go** you keep friendships and save yourself from carrying around poisonous anger that hurts no one but yourself.

So are you ready for a little practice in **forgiving and letting go?**

Grab a roll of toilet paper and a marker. Write down every grudge you are holding from the time your dog used your bed for a bathroom to the grudge you are holding against your best friend for hurting your feelings.

Write out one grudge per piece of toilet paper. (If you fill the whole roll, you really needed this exercise!) When you are done, toss them in that porcelain throne (the toilet that is) and flush them away! (Just not all at once. Yikes!)

OPPOSITE DAY

Run with scissors.
Leave your lights on.
Don't put your toys away!
Call out the answer before raising your hand.
Don't look at me when I'm talking to you.

These statements are probably the *exact opposite* of what you are used to hearing. In fact, you are so used to being told the opposite of these things, you could probably reverse those statements in your sleep.

Because there are just some things we all grow up hearing a million times.

This isn't a new thing. Over two thousand years ago, the people who lived on Earth while Jesus was walking around had statements like this as well. Things they could recite in their sleep and had heard since they were small kids. Things like . . .

Keep the Sabbath holy.
Worship no other gods.
Honor your father and mother.

One day, Jesus was speaking to a group of His followers and made a statement—a commandment—that was the *exact opposite* of what everyone in the crowd had grown up hearing. Jesus's words are found in the book of Matthew:

> "You have heard that it was said, 'Love your neighbor. Hate your enemy.' But here is what I tell you. Love your enemies. Pray for those who hurt you."
> (Matthew 5:43-44)

Love your enemies.

It's not as shocking to us today because, in that moment, Jesus changed the way we look at our enemies. In a time when everyone grew up thinking it was best to hate your enemies, to seek revenge on your enemies, Jesus said the exact opposite. Two thousand years later, His words still ring true.

Be kind to those who aren't kind to you.

It's not easy. But it's worth it. In the end, if you can **be kind to those who aren't kind to you,** you will be happier and have fewer enemies. Because here's a secret . . . are you ready?

It's no fun to be mean to someone who is kind to you.

Jesus knows this. He knows that *love changes everything*. And when you treat someone kindly, when you show love to everyone—even those who are mean to you—everything changes.

It changes the way you see your enemies.
It changes the way your enemies see you.
It changes the way your enemies treat you.

Do you have any enemies? Is there anyone in your life who isn't always kind to you?

....

....

....

....

What do they do to you that is unkind?

....

....

....

....

How have you responded in the past?

....

....

....

....

What are some ways you could **be kind to those who aren't kind to you?**

....

....

....

....

ONE IS THE LONELIEST NUMBER

Some things in life are difficult to do all on your own.
Some things are downright impossible to do alone.

What are a few things that just wouldn't be the same if you were to try to do them on your own?

....

....

....

Well, here's the great news: God didn't make you to go through life on your own. Sure, there may be days when everyone is busy and you find yourself sitting all alone at the bottom of a see-saw. (Actually, if you ever find yourself in that situation, stand up and get on the swings or go for a walk. At least find something you *can* do on your own.)

Anyway, God made us to help each other through this life. He made us to live in community, surrounded by friends, family, classmates, teammates, and neighbors.

Why?

Because God knows when life is awesome, it's even more awesome to be able to share and celebrate that awesomeness with others.

And God also knows when life is really bad, it's easier to make it through the bad days when you are surrounded by others.

Who are some of the people you celebrate good days with and lean on through the bad days?

....

....

....

Now let's flip it around. Sure, you need people to celebrate with. And you need people to lean on.

But who needs to lean on you?

Just like you need the community of your friends and family, they need you as well. They need you to celebrate with them when they succeed. But more importantly, they need you to help them through the difficult days.

The day they lose their math book before a big test.
The day they get in trouble for being disrespectful.
The day their grandma gets sick.
The day they have to put their dog to sleep.

Some things in life are downright impossible to go through alone.

Check out what the Bible tells us about how to be a good friend in the hard times:

> **"Carry one another's heavy loads. If you do, you will fulfill the law of Christ."** *(Galatians 6:2)*

There are people in your life who are carrying some heavy loads. (No, not like they tried to cram one too many textbooks in their backpacks. Although, I'm sure if you offered to carry a load like that, it would be appreciated.)

This verse is talking about the loads that are heavy on our hearts. Things like . . .

broken relationships,
sickness,
poverty,
loneliness.
These are *really* heavy things for someone to carry all alone.

That's why it's important to **look for ways to help others.** Maybe one of your close friends is carrying a heavy load. Maybe it's one of your family members. Or maybe it is just someone in your school or church who is carrying something heavy. Whoever it is, God tells us to love others by **looking for ways to help others.**

What what are some difficult situations you have seen people go through?

....

....

....

What could you do to help make those difficult times feel a little lighter?

....

....

....

....

....

This week you learned a little more about how God's love changes your relationships.

God's love changes the way you treat others.
God's love changes the way you use your words.
God's love changes the way you forgive.
God's love changes the way you treat your enemies.
God's love changes the way you respond to people who are hurting.

God's love changes everything!

Use what you learned this week to write someone a letter. (Yes, with a pen and paper. And with an envelope, address and stamp!)

Maybe you thought of someone you need to treat more kindly. Maybe there's someone who needs encouragement, someone who needs your complete forgiveness, someone who is hurting and struggling to carry a heavy load, maybe even someone you considered your enemy.

Use the space on the next page to write a letter to that person. It could be a letter that starts mending a broken relationship. It could be a letter of encouragement. Or it could be simply telling a funny story that will make someone smile.

Then tear up your letter, slip it in an envelope, address it, and stamp it. Send it off in the mail (even if the recipient of the letter lives in your house!).

WEEK FOUR

INTRODUCTION

God's love changes everything.

How many times have you read that sentence over the last three weeks?

You started off reading the incredible story of God's love through the life, death, and resurrection of Jesus.

You went on to learn how God's love changes the way you look at yourself and the decisions you make.

Then, last week, you read the many ways God's love changes the way you treat others.

So what's left?

Only the most important piece: *How you treat God.*

Sure, God's love changes everything but . . .
How do you feel that love?
How can your entire life be changed by a relationship with someone you *can't see*?
How do you **love God** back?

This week, we are going to talk about the last piece of that verse found in Luke that we have been focusing on. The one that tells us all we know about how Jesus grew up. Here's a refresher:

> Jesus became wiser and stronger. He also became more and more pleasing to God and to people. (Luke 2:52)

You know how to grow stronger (eat your veggies).

You've learned how to grow wiser (week 2).

We've talked about how to become more pleasing to people (last week).

Now it's time to talk about the last (and maybe biggest) piece of the puzzle: How to become more pleasing to God.

LOOKING FOR THE INVISIBLE

Have you ever seen the wind?

Have you ever actually seen it rushing towards you off the ocean? Or the wind slamming against the side of city skyscrapers?

Of course not.

No one can actually *see* the wind. But if you . . .

fly kites,
wind surf,
paraglide,
sail,
or live in one of the 18 million homes powered by wind turbines...

then you have *definitely* seen what wind can do.

Even if none of those apply to you, you have seen trees and plants sway, heard stories of tornadoes and hurricanes destroying towns, or even watched balloons bob and float into the sky.

No one has ever *seen* the wind. But . . . we have all seen what wind can do.

God is a lot like the wind. We cannot see God but we have all seen what God can do. And just like we believe wind exists because we see all that it does, we believe God exists because we have seen all He does.

**Faith is believing in what you can't see
because of what you can see.**

We have faith in a God we can't see because we can see . . .

> . . . His magnificent creation—the sky, mountains, ocean plains—all around us.
> . . . His love in the way others love us.
> . . . the way we serve others because of His love for us.

Check out what the book of Hebrews tells us about faith:

Faith is being sure of what we hope for. It is being sure of what we do not see. *(Hebrews 11:1)*

It's no secret that God is invisible. Other than the short 33 years Jesus walked this earth, God has always been sort of invisible.

Yet, there have been generations after generations,
hundreds of millions of people,
entire countries and people groups,
who believe in a God they cannot see.

Why?

Because they saw Him:

set fire to a bush that didn't burn,
turn water into blood,
cover an entire country with frogs,
make a dry path in the middle of the ocean,
make bread fall from the sky,
cause strong walls to crumble,
resurrect a man from the dead.

Just to name a few.

So how can you have faith in a God you can't see? How can you have a relationship with someone you cannot touch or hear? Because of all the things you *can* see, touch, and hear because of God.

> **Faith is believing in what you can't see because of what you can see.**

Take a few minutes to list some things you *can* see that point back to or help you believe in a God you *can't* see:

....

....

....

....

....

....

....

....

....

....

....

....

....

....

SUPERNATURAL LION TAMER

Do you know anyone who seems as if they can do anything?

Write the letter from column A in the correct blank in column B.

COLUMN A   COLUMN B

A. Doctor . . .   Can predict the weather

B. Soldier . . .   Can heal the sick

C. Firefighter . . .   Can feed people

D. Chef . . .   Can defeat armies

E. Artist . . .   Can turn objects into animals

F. Magician . . .   Can paint sunsets

G. Weatherman . . .   Can save people from a fire

H. Lion Tamer . . .   Can control lions

Those are a lot of talents. Would you believe it if I told you there was someone who was actually an expert in all the career paths listed in Column A (plus a few dozen more)? Not only that, but that this someone outshines all the best doctors, soldiers, chefs, or artists?

Well, grab a Bible (or open your Bible app) and read a few of the following scriptures:

> Luke 17:11-14
> Joshua 10:12-13
> Daniel 3:19-27
> Matthew 14:15-21
> Genesis 1:3-5
> Exodus 7:8-10
> 1 Samuel 12:18
> Daniel 6:16-23

As it turns out, you *do* know someone who can do anything. Someone who can heal the sick, protect people from a fire, and calm hungry lions better than any doctor, firefighter, or lion tamer the world has ever seen!

God can do anything.

The Bible is full of story after story of God proving He can be trusted. And because we know God can do anything, we know we can trust Him completely. Check out this verse found in the book of Jeremiah:

> **"Lord and King, you have reached out your great and powerful arm. You have made the heavens and the earth. Nothing is too hard for you."** *(Jeremiah 32:17)*

Nothing is too hard for God. Nothing.

Your grades in school.
Making new friends after moving across the country.
Getting along with your sister.
Your parents' divorce.
Your aunt's sickness.

God has made all the heavens and all the earth. God has proven Himself over and over. Nothing is too hard for God.

You can trust God because He can do anything.

Sometimes this is a difficult truth for us to believe. It's difficult because sometimes, God doesn't do what we want. And we ask, if God *can* do anything, why *doesn't* He do this one thing?

Take a few minutes to write out one situation in your life right now or in the past in which you felt this way—one time you wondered if God really could do anything because He didn't do what you wanted:

....

....

....

....

....

....

....

....

....

....

....

Over the next few days we will talk more about God's power and why He may or may not do what we want. But for today, spend a few minutes talking with God about the time you just wrote about. Ask Him why. Spill out your feelings to Him. And if you can, tell Him you know you can still **trust Him because He can do anything.**

THE BEST LAID PLANS

Would you rather (circle one) . . .

. . . use eyedrops made of vinegar **OR** toilet paper made of sandpaper?

. . . have a dragon **OR** be a dragon?

. . . wear a snowsuit in the desert **OR** wear a swimsuit in Antarctica?

. . . win a trip to Hawaii **OR** win a free laptop?

. . . have bad breath **OR** have smelly feet?

. . . let your life go as YOU plan **OR** let your life go as GOD plans?

Listen. This is a devotion. A Christian devotion. About God. I know you circled the second option on that last question, but do you really think that?

What if your plan is to get really famous and make tons of money?
What if your plan is to cure cancer *and* be the first person to walk on Mars?
What if your plan is really, really great?

Check out this passage from the book of Isaiah:

> "My thoughts are not like your thoughts. And your ways are not like my ways," announces the Lord. "The heavens are higher than the earth. And my ways are higher than your ways. My thoughts are higher than your thoughts."
> *(Isaiah 55:8-9)*

God is God. He knows more than me. He knows more than you. He knows more than the smartest person to have ever lived.

He knows if you get famous, you'll hate all the paparazzi.

He knows if you make tons of money, you'll lose all your best friends.

He knows if you devote your life to cancer research or interplanetary travel, you will miss out on spending the best years of your life as a missionary.

In the end, **God's plan is always better than your plan.**

Can you think of a time in your life when things didn't go according to your plan (like a move, a friendship, a vacation, etc.), but after a while, things turned out okay or even better? Write what happened here:

....

....

....

....

....

Sometimes things don't happen the way we plan. And sometimes we can look back months or years later and see that even though things didn't go as we'd planned, it turned out better.

Then there are times when things don't go according to our plan that we will never understand in our lifetime.

That's usually when BIG things don't go according to our plan.

Sickness.
Death.
A fire.
A flood.

Those kinds of things can make us wonder if God's plan really is better. But here's what we don't realize:

God never promises His plan will be better just for you and me . . .

God's plan is better *for God*.

God's plan is better for getting the most amount of people in a relationship with Him.

God's plan is better for bringing His kingdom to earth.

God's plan is better for His story.

Sometimes God's plan turns out way better for us. And sometimes we won't understand God's plan until we sit next to Him in Heaven. Either way, the Bible says **you can trust God because His plan is better than your plan.**

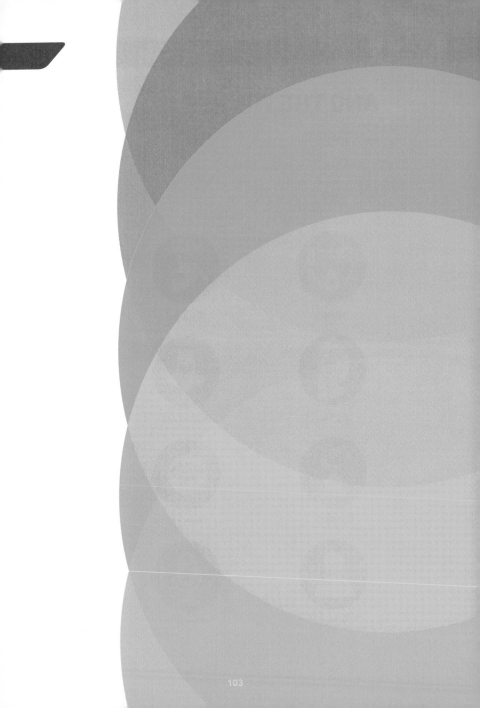

AND THE WINNER IS...

Who do you think would win in a fight? (Draw a big X through the loser on each row):

BEAR   SHARK

ELSA   BATMAN

PIRATE   NINJA

YOU   SIRI

There are a lot of powerful people and characters in the world. Maybe we wonder whose powers are the best. We debate and try to figure out who is the most powerful and who would win in a fight.

And we want that person or character on our side. Why?
Because . . .
A bear is more powerful than you.
Batman is more powerful than you.
A ninja is more powerful than you.

We all want to feel as though we are being protected by something more powerful than us.

But did you know you have the most powerful being already on your side?

Of course you do!

Because for the past two days, you've read and learned about all the incredible things God has made and done.

From sunsets to thunderstorms.
From angry frogs to tame lions.
From lunch for thousands to healing for ten.
God has proven His power over and over.

He is more powerful than sharks, pirates and Elsa . . . combined. But most importantly, God is more powerful than *you*.

And that's all the reason you really need to put your faith and trust in Him.

God can do *anything*.
God knows *everything*.
God is *all-powerful*.

DAY 4

In the book of 1 Corinthians, Paul tells the new Christians why God's power is so important to our faith:

> I didn't preach my message with clever and compelling words. Instead, my preaching showed the Holy Spirit's power. This was so that your faith would be based on God's power. Your faith would not be based on human wisdom.
> *(1 Corinthians 2:4-5)*

Paul is saying that our faith should be based on God's power alone. Paul is saying that it's because of God's power, not Paul's words, that Christianity spread throughout the world after Jesus came back from the dead.

It's because of God's power you are still hearing (and living) His Story today. And it's because of God's power that you can trust Him no matter what.

Who do you think would win in a fight? (Draw a big X through the loser):

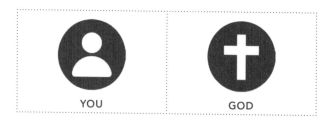

YOU   GOD

You can trust God because He is more powerful than you.

(Side note: Anyone who has accidentally dropped an iPhone on concrete or left their phone in their swim trunks knows you would definitely win in a fight against Siri.)

SUPER POWER

Did you know . . .

- . . . several drops of Super Glue can hold a two-ton truck in the air?
- . . . Super Glue can be used in place of stitches to heal a wound?
- . . . if you were lost in the woods in need of heat, you could put cotton on Super Glue to make a fire?
- . . . people have accidentally glued their fingers, eyelids and lips together with Super Glue?
- . . . you should *always* have an adult present before you use Super Glue?

Super Glue is some powerful stuff. And when you use it, no amount of pulling, tugging or prying will ever separate what you glued together.

Did you know, God's love for you is a lot like Super Glue?

It's easy to feel as if love is something that is conditional.

You love your sister . . . as long as she doesn't break your new game.

Your mom loves your dog . . . as long as he doesn't poop on the kitchen floor again.

Your coach loves you . . . as long as you make the winning goal.

But God's love is completely unconditional. God loves you *no matter what*. And just like Super Glue, there is *nothing* that can separate you from God's love.

Read these verses found in the book of Romans:

> Who can separate us from Christ's love? Can trouble or hard times or harm or hunger? Can nakedness or danger or war? It is written, "Because of you, we face death all day long. We are considered as sheep to be killed." No! In all these things we are more than winners! We owe it all to Christ, who has loved us. I am absolutely sure that not even death or life can separate us from God's love. Not even angels or demons, the present or the future, or any powers can separate us. Not even the highest places or the lowest, or anything else in all creation can separate us. Nothing at all can ever separate us from God's love. That's because of what Christ Jesus our Lord has done.
> *(Romans 8:35-39)*

Okay, okay so God's love isn't *exactly* like Super Glue. Super Glue can at least be separated with a little nail polish remover. God's love is even stronger than Super Glue.

But why is that so important?

You can trust God because He loves you no matter what.

So far this week, you have heard that you can trust God because He can do anything, His plan is better than yours and He is more powerful than you. But . . . without His love, all of that is meaningless.

Why would you trust someone who was powerful but didn't love you at all? Why would you believe in someone who had a great plan but didn't care at all about you?

That's where God's love changes everything.

Not only is He powerful, not only can He do anything, not only are His plans greater, **God loves you no matter what**. *Nothing* can separate you from His love.

And that is why you can put your trust in Him. That is why you can believe and have faith in the all-powerful God who loves *you*. If you weren't ready to put your trust in God and start a relationship with Jesus after week one but feel like you know enough to accept God's life-changing gift of love now, turn back to page 32 and follow the steps in the What's Next section.

This week you learned a few BIG reasons you can trust our BIG God, no matter what.

So take a few minutes to create this unique pinwheel that will spin in the wind and remind you of all the reasons to trust God. Because faith is believing in what you can't see because of what you can see. (Like believing in the wind because you see this pinwheel spinning!)

MATERIALS:

- Scissors
- 1 wooden dowel
- 2-3 small beads
- 1 thumbtack
- This sheet of paper

1. Tear out the square on page 113.

2. Fold the paper along the crisscrossed lines.

3. Cut the paper from each of the four corners until the dotted line stops.

4. Pull _every other_ tip to the middle so there are four points left out and four points held together in the center.

5. Push your thumbtack through the center of the four points.

6. Flip your pinwheel over to make sure the tack pokes in the middle. You can move the thumbtack around to make the hole a little larger.

7. Slip two or three small beads on the back of the thumbtack before sticking it into your wooden dowel.

8. Place your pinwheel in the ground outside or tape your dowel to the outside of your window so you can watch it spin in the wind.

Be reminded of what you can't see because of what you can see!

GOD CAN
DO ANYTHING

GOD'S PLAN
IS BETTER
THAN MINE

GOD LOVES ME
NO MATTER WHAT

GOD IS MORE
POWERFUL
THAN ME